THE ROAD TO SARAJEVO

THE ROAD TO SARAJEVO

Origins of the
First World War

Harry Mills

MACMILLAN
EDUCATION

Books by the same author:
The Way We Were
Britain, Europe and Beyond
Digging Up the Past
Twentieth Century World History in Focus

First published in New Zealand in 1983 by
THE MACMILLAN COMPANY OF NEW ZEALAND LTD

First published in Great Britain in 1986 by
MACMILLAN EDUCATION LTD
Houndmills, Basingstoke, Hampshire RG21 2XS
and London
Companies and representatives
throughout the world

Printed in Hong Kong

ISBN 0-333-43825-6

CONTENTS

Introduction

The aim of *The Road To Sarajevo* is to combine the best of the modern resource-based history with a straightforward narrative text.

Every chapter starts with a concise, clearly written introductory narrative which is then supported and extended by pictorial and written resources on the following pages.

The questions on the resources, and the ideas for further work are designed to encourage pupils to recall, assess, compare and contrast the evidence. As well as helping students to develop the skills of historical enquiry and judgement, the questions focus attention on the importance and reliability of evidence.

In addition, review chapters focus on the historiography of the causes of the First World War, calling for an intelligent evaluation of the latest research.

In short, the aim has been to combine the best of modern and traditional methods.

★   ★   ★

Read the following before starting on this text.

Most of the questions in this book are followed by bracketed letters, e.g. (A), (B) referring to resources such as extracts, drawings, photographs and maps. Sometimes you will have to refer to a number of different resources to answer a single question. For example, if a question was followed by (C) (D) (E), you would need to refer to the three resources to answer the question properly.

1 – The Roots of Strife

*Bismarck maintains peace and protects Germany by isolating
France through a network of alliances.*

The Birth of Germany

The roots of the First World War go back to the birth of modern Germany. Until the 1860s Germany was little more than a loose collection of states. Then between 1864 and 1871, Prussia, the largest and most powerful of the German states, fought and won three wars to bring the weaker German states under her control. First, in 1864, Prussia combined with Austria to seize the northern states of Schleswig and Holstein. Next, in 1866, Prussia overwhelmed Austria in seven weeks, destroying Austria's hopes of ever leading the German states. The resulting North German Confederation united all of northern Germany under Prussian leadership. Lastly, in 1870-71, Prussia defeated France and seized the French provinces of Alsace and Lorraine. The South German states now united with Prussia to form a single German nation.

The new Germany was in effect an enlarged Prussia. The Prussian King Wilhelm I was crowned Kaiser (Emperor) while his Chief Minister Bismarck became Chancellor (Prime Minister).

Bismarck's Alliances

Bismarck had in fact, masterminded Germany's unification. Now he was determined to protect his creation. A united state of over 40 million Germans in the heart of Europe was bound to be feared and distrusted. France, especially, would never forget the humiliation of 1870-71 and the loss of Alsace and Lorraine. If France was ever able to ally itself with a powerful neighbour then Germany's very existence would be threatened. The thrust of Bismarck's foreign policy was therefore to isolate France.

To isolate France, Bismarck constructed an elaborate network of alliances. Bismarck's success can be judged by looking at the most important of these.

In 1873 Bismarck bound the rulers of Austria and Russia to Germany in a treaty of friendship called the **Dreikaiserbund** or **League of the Three Emperors.** Their governments would consult each other on matters of mutual interest; and more importantly they would maintain friendly neutrality in case any one of them should be attacked by another power. But when Austria-Hungary and Russia quarrelled over the Balkans, the league crumbled and by 1878 it was dead.

(A)   AU REVOIR!
                    Germany: 'Farewell, Madam, and if —'
                    France: 'Ha! We shall meet again!'
                         (*Punch*, 27 September 1873)

Under the terms of peace treaty following France's defeat in 1871, France was forced to pay Germany compensation of £200,000,000 and to accept a German army of occupation until the money was paid. The German troops finally left in 1873.

To replace it Bismarck drew up the secret **Dual Alliance** with Austria in 1879. It was a defensive alliance whereby Germany and Austria agreed to help each other if attacked by Russia. Three years later in 1882, Italy joined to turn it into the **Triple Alliance.**

9

In 1881 Bismarck managed to revive the Three Emperors League, but in 1887 when it came up for its three yearly renewal the Russians refused to sign. Once again differences over the Balkans had turned Russia and Austria into bitter rivals. Nevertheless Bismarck was still able to bind Russia to Germany in a separate alliance — the **Reinsurance Treaty** of 1887.

All this time Bismarck worked hard to stay friends with Britain. As a result of this brilliant diplomacy, all the mainland powers of Europe except France were now tied to Germany in a network of alliances. No longer did there seem any danger of Germany being encircled by a ring of enemies. France was isolated, friendless and therefore powerless.

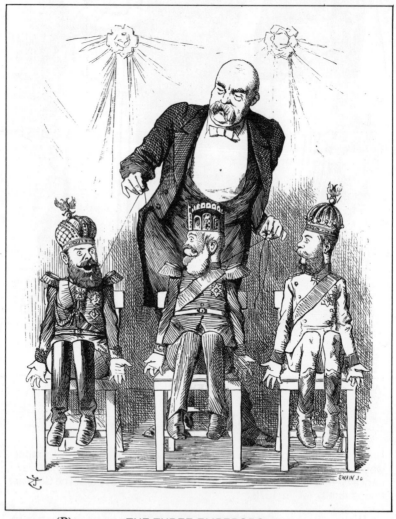

(B)   THE THREE EMPERORS –
Or, The Ventriloquist of Varzin!

A Punch cartoon on the Three Emperors' League (1881).

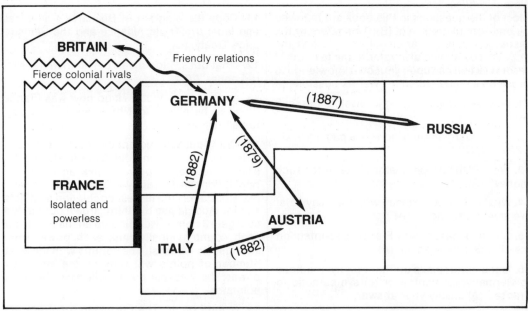

(C)

(D)

REVANCHISM

The French never forgot their humiliating defeat by Prussia in 1870-71. The desire for *la revanche* or revenge remained alive until the First World War.

Victor Hugo spoke for most Frenchmen when he wrote:

'France will have one thought: to reconstitute her forces, gather her energy, nourish her sacred anger, raise her generation to form an army of the whole people, to work without cease, to study the methods and skills of our enemies to become again a great France, the France of 1792, the France of an idea with a sword. Then one day she will be irresistable. Then she will take back Alsace-Lorraine.'

(B. Tuchman, *August 1914*)

(E)

THE STRENGTH OF THE EUROPEAN POWERS IN 1900						
	Austria-Hungary	France	Germany	Great Britain	Italy	Russia
Population	45,015,000	38,641,333	56,367,176	41,605,323	32,450,000	132,960,000
Men in regular army	397,316	589,541	585,266	280,733	261,728	860,000
Annual iron & steel production (tons)	2,580,000	3,250,000	13,790,000	13,860,000	500,000	5,015,000
Annual value of foreign trade (£)	151,599,000	460,408,000	545,205,000	877,448,917	132,970,000	141,799,000
Merchant fleet (net tonnage)	313,698	1,037,720	1,941,645	9,304,108	945,000	633,820
1st class battleships	6	13	14	38	9	13
2nd class battleships	6	10	14	11	5	10

11

ACTIVITIES

Note carefully:

Most of the questions in this book are followed by bracketed letters, e.g. (B). This refers to the resource where you are most likely to find the answer. You should also refer to the text, other resources and call upon your own knowledge to provide as complete an answer as possible.

1. Why is Germany saying farewell to France? (A)

2. Why is Germany leaving with a bag marked £200,000,000? (A)

3. What is the proper historical term for such money? (A)

4. What does France mean when she says 'Ha! We shall meet again!' (A)

5. Give two reasons why France is so intent on meeting Germany again. (A)

6. Is the cartoonist's attitude: (a) sympathetic to Germany, (b) neutral or (c) sympathetic to France? (A) Justify your answer.

7. Identify the countries of the three Emperors in the cartoon? (B)

8. Why is Bismarck portrayed as a ventriloquist? (B)

9. What point is the cartoonist making about the Three Emperors' League? (B)

10. Do you think the cartoon is an accurate comment on Bismarck's abilities as a diplomat? (C) Justify your answer.

11. Copy the diagram of Bismarck's alliances and label the Triple Alliance and the Reinsurance Treaty. (C)

12. What does Hugo mean by 'nourish her sacred anger'? (D)

13. According to Victor Hugo how was France going to be able to get back Alsace and Lorraine? (D)

14. Copy out and complete the table below. Using the information from (E), indicate on a 1-6 scale where each power ranks according to population, size of army and so on. For example, Russia has the largest population so it gets 1 point. Austria has the third largest population so it gets 3 points. Now add up all the points for each country. Finally rank each power from strongest to weakest. The country with the least number of points will rank as the strongest power; the weakest power will have the most points.

15. *Talking point:* The European great powers were the largest, richest and most populous states. Moreover they had to be able to defend their great power status in battle.

Italy saw herself as a great power, but it was only after 1882, as an ally to the Central Power of Germany and Austria-Hungary, that she could claim anything like equality with the other two nations.

What evidence is there in the table to support this statement?

THE STRENGTH OF THE EUROPEAN POWERS IN 1900					
	Austria-Hungary	France	Germany	Great Britain	Italy	Russia
Population						
Army						
Iron & steel						
Trade						
Merchant fleet						
Battleships						
Points						
Ranking						

2 – Germany's Quest For World Power

The new German Kaiser Wilhelm II dismisses Bismarck and embarks on a drive for world power.

The Fall of Bismarck

For 20 years Germany enjoyed peace and security under Bismarck. Most Europeans were convinced that Germany was a contented, peace-loving nation which would only fight in self-defence.

All this changed after Wilhelm II was crowned Kaiser in 1888. Vain, arrogant and unpredictable, Wilhelm clashed with Bismarck on virtually everything. While Bismarck wanted Germany to stay as a land-based European power, Wilhelm wanted Germany to follow a world policy or **Weltpolitik.** This meant turning Germany into a world power with a large colonial empire.

In 1890 Wilhelm forced Bismarck to resign. Disaster soon followed. Within days, the Kaiser was persuaded not to renew the Reinsurance Treaty with Russia, leaving the way clear for an anti-German alliance. Russia turned to France and in 1894 they signed the ~~Dual Entente.~~ Both sides promised to fight side by side if attacked by Germany. *Franco-Russia[n]*

Bismarck's worst fears had come true. France's isolation had ended. Five of Europe's Great Powers were now split into two rival camps.

German Economic Growth

Wilhelm had good cause to feel Germany deserved world power status. Germany's economy was booming. In industrial and steel production, Germany rapidly overhauled Great Britain until, by 1913, she was second only to the USA.

Colonial Expansion

To continue economic expansion, German industrialists and traders argued that Germany had to become a great colonial power. Colonies provided secure markets and raw materials. Influential pressure groups such as the German Colonial and Pan German League churned out a stream of pro-colonial propaganda. Without colonies, they claimed, Germany would become a second-rate power. What was good enough for England, they argued, was good enough for Germany.

For Wilhelm, an empire would bring the added prestige and respect he so desperately wanted.

But Germany's bid for colonial greatness was doomed; Germans had started too late in the race for colonies. All that remained were a few Pacific islands and some worthless tracts in Africa. To cover up the frustration, meagre gains were hailed as great prizes. When Germany won the tiny Caroline Islands, Chancellor Bülow proclaimed to the Kaiser:

'This gain will prompt the people and navy to follow Your Majesty further along the way leading to world power, greatness and eternal glory.'

Naval Expansion

A world power needed a large navy. In 1896 Wilhelm announced the 'future of Germany was on the sea'. The next year, Admiral von Tirpitz, one of the strongest supports of Weltpolitik, became Secretary of the Navy. Tirpitz dreamed of Germany as a great naval power. Through a series of naval laws he began to turn the navy from a coastal protection force into a battle fleet capable of challenging the might of the British Navy.

(A)

TABLE 1

Population (millions)

Year (approx.) in some cases	USA	Great Britain	Germany	France	Russia
1870	39.9	26.1	41.1	36.1	84.5
1900	76.1	37.0	56.4	38.5	132.9
1910	92.4	40.8	64.9	39.2	160.7

TABLE 2

Share of World Industrial Production (percentages)

	USA	Great Britain	Germany	France	Russia	All Others
1870	23	32	13	10	4	18
1896-1900	30	20	17	7	5	21
1913	36	14	16	6	6	22

TABLE 3

Share of World Trade (percentages)

	USA	Great Britain	Germany	France	Russia	All Others
1870	8	25	10	10	5	42
1901-05	11	16	12	7	4	50
1913	11	16	12	7	n/a	54*

*includes Russia

(B)

GERMANY'S COLONIAL MISSION

Within Germany, powerful pressure groups such as the German Colonial and Pan German Leagues agitated for Germany to expand.

In 1896 historian Hans Delbruck wrote:

'In the next decades vast tracts of land in very different parts of the world will be distributed. The nation which goes away empty-handed will lose its place in the next generation from the ranks of those Great Powers which will coin the human spirit. Did we found the German Empire to see it disappear under our grandchildren?'

In 1899 he proclaimed:

'We want to be a World Power and pursue colonial policy in the grand manner. That is certain. Here there can be no step backward. The entire future of our people among the great nations depends on it. We can pursue this policy with England or without England. With England means in peace; against England means — through war.'

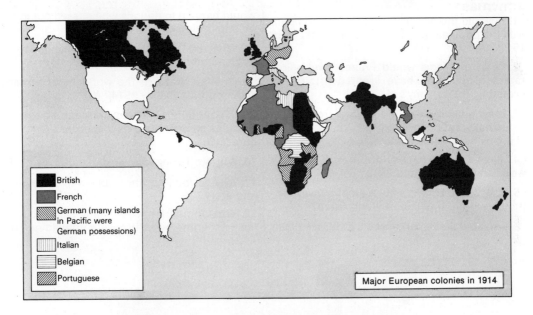

British

French

German (many islands in Pacific were German possessions)

Italian

Belgian

Portuguese

Major European colonies in 1914

(D) THE MAJOR COLONIAL POWERS OF EUROPE: 1914

	Colonial area in sq. miles (M)	Number of Colonial Territories
Britain	12+	55
France	4+	29
Germany	1+	10
Belgium Portugal Netherlands Italy	3	21

(E)

TIRPITZ AND THE GERMAN NAVY

The driving force behind the expanding German Navy was the Secretary of the Navy, Admiral von Tirpitz.

Publicly the German people were told the navy was for the 'protection of sea trade and colonies'.

In a private memorandum marked 'very secret', Tirpitz wrote:

'For Germany the most dangerous naval enemy at the present time is England. It is also the enemy against which we most urgently require a certain measure of naval force as a political power factor.'

The idea of a powerful navy won the support of the Pan-German League and Colonial Union. Tirpitz won the support of the business classes who stood to gain by huge orders for steel and guns. The industrialist Krupp provided funds to found a Naval League to mobilise public support which rapidly grew to a membership of a million people.

ACTIVITIES

1. How did the population of France compare with the population of Germany in: (a) 1870, (b) 1910? (A)

2. What problems would France's very slow rate of population have created for: (a) its economy, (b) its army? (A)

3. Draw a list ranking the powers from 1-5 in industrial production in: (a) 1870, (b) 1913. What changes have taken place? (A)

4. Where did Britain and Germany rank in world trade in 1870 and 1913? (A)

5. How would Britain's huge empire have contributed to her position in world trade?

6. What did the historian Hans Delbruck claim would happen to nations who missed out in the race for colonies? (B)

7. What did Delbruck suggest would happen if England stood in Germany's way? (B)

8. In what areas of the world had Germany acquired colonies by 1914? (C)

9. In your opinion, could Germany's quest for colonies be described as a success? Quote figures. (D)

10. Why did Tirpitz want an expanded navy? (E)

11. Why do you think the public was told a different story? (E)

12. What industries in Germany stood to gain the most from a boom in naval shipbuilding? (E)

3 – The End of British Isolation

Britain ends her isolation. The big powers of Europe split into two armed camps – the Triple Alliance and the Triple Entente.

The initial reaction in Britain to Germany's naval programme was surprisingly mild. Britain had always looked to her navy to protect her empire and the trade routes to it. Indeed it was British policy to have a fleet that was the equal to any two navies in the world put together.

Britain Looks for an Ally

But in the late 1890 s Britain had other worries. For the previous 30 years she had tried to keep out of European affairs. Instead she preferred to concentrate on looking after her vast empire; pursuing a policy of 'splendid isolation'. But isolation was no longer safe. Britain's two chief colonial rivals, France and Russia, had combined in 1894 to form the Dual Entente. To counter this Britain needed an ally. For most Britons, Germany seemed the best choice. Germany, however never overcame its suspicions of a British ulterior motive and the discussions of an alliance came to nothing. So Britain turned elsewhere. To gain help in the event of a war with Russia, Britain signed a treaty in 1902 with Japan — the **Anglo Japanese Alliance.**

The Entente Cordiale

Next, Britain decided to patch up some of her colonial differences with her traditional enemy, France. King Edward VII paved the way with a highly successful state visit to Paris in 1903. In 1904, an Entente Cordiale was signed. France said that Britain could have a free hand in Egypt. In return Britain gave France a free hand in Morocco.

In itself the Entente Cordiale was nothing more than a friendly understanding. It was not a military alliance. Britain had no wish to get involved in any continental war. Yet the Germans behaved as if it was an anti-German alliance.

Because of this, the Germans were determined to break up the entente. Germany therefore deliberately provoked a quarrel with France.

The First Moroccan Crisis, 1905

In 1905, the German Kaiser paid a visit to the Moroccan port of Tangier. There he declared that Morocco should be independent of France. Germany calculated that in the crisis that was sure to follow, Britain would refuse to back France. The entente would then collapse. For a time it looked as though the German plan would succeed. Delcasse, the French Foreign Minister responsible for the Entente Cordiale, was forced to resign following a conspiracy of his cabinet colleagues who were under German pressure. But then at the Algeciras Conference in 1906, set up to solve the crisis, the German plan back-fired. By threatening war over Morocco, Germany pushed Britain and France closer together. Instead of collapsing, the entente hardened. Britain backed France and Germany suffered a diplomatic defeat.

Algeciras was a disastrous setback for Germany. The entente was stronger than ever; diplomatic and public opinion turned against Germany, while military talks between the British and French armed forces were initiated as a precautionary measure.

Algeciras also exposed a weakness in the Triple Alliance when Italy deserted Germany and backed France. From now on the Germans would grumble that Austria was their only true friend in Europe.

To make matters worse, Germany's action pushed Britain into reaching an understanding with Russia. In the Anglo-Russian Entente of 1907, Britain and Russia settled their differences over Afghanistan, Tibet and Persia.

The Triple Entente

Britain was now linked to both France and Russia, thereby creating the Triple Entente. Europe was divided into two camps, with the Triple Entente on one side and the Triple Alliance on the other.

After the Triple Entente was formed, Germany complained more and more of being encircled by a ring of hostile nations whose aim was to deny it a share of world power.

This was not true. Nevertheless, the existence of two rival camps increased suspicion and fear. Moreover, they meant that a war between two nations was likely to involve many others.

(A)
Britannia to Colonia: 'After all, my dear, we needn't trouble ourselves about the others.'
Colonia replies: 'No, we can always dance together you and I.'

(*Punch*, 1901)

18

(B) THE MATCH-MAKER MALGRE ELLE

Mlle. La France (*aside*): 'If she's going to glare at us like that, it almost looks as if we might have to be regularly engaged.'

(*Punch,* 12 April 1905)

(C) WHY NOT?

France (to Russia): 'Aren't you going to dance with Mr Bull?'

Russia: 'I think I should rather like to, if he wouldn't tread on my toes.'

France: 'Oh, but he won't. He's improved immensely. I find him adorable!'

(*Punch,* 11 October 1905)

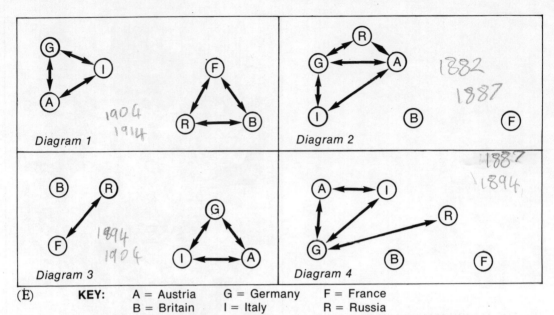

KEY: A = Austria   G = Germany   F = France
B = Britain   I = Italy   R = Russia

The diagram represents the pattern of alliances and ententes at various dates between 1882 and 1908. Countries with alliances or ententes are joined together.

(D)

THE MOROCCAN CRISIS THROUGH GERMAN EYES

(i) In 1904, one German newspaper reported:

'Morocco is a German concern owing to our increasing population and need of naval bases. If Germany does not peg out claims, she will retire empty-handed from the partition of the world. Is the German man-in-the street to get nothing? The time has come when Germany must secure Morocco . . .'

(ii) The German pressure group, the Pan German League was very upset at the Entente Cordiale claiming it was:

'[an insult] to the German Empire to have been overlooked in the [talks] between Britain and France on the future of Morocco . . . [Germany has] been treated as a third-rate power.'

(iii) The reaction of the German government to the Entente Cordiale was just as strong. Baroness von Spitzenberg who had contacts in the German Foreign Office wrote in her diary:

'There is deep gloom at the Foreign Ministry over the Franco-British agreement on Morocco. [It is] one of the worst defeats of German policy since the Dual [Entente between France and Russia]'.

(iv) Holstein, an important Foreign Office official, later told a friend that Great Britain's entente with France had convinced him that:

'Before the rings of other Great Powers tightens around us, we must attempt with all our energies and with a determination that will not shrink from the utmost to break the ring. Hence the Tangier trip of the [Kaiser]!'

ACTIVITIES

1. Which country or group of countries is represented by: (a) Britannia, (b) Colonia, (c) the soldier standing alone, (d) the ladies dancing in the background, (e) the gentleman dancing in the background? (A)

2. Why didn't Britannia and Colonia want to 'trouble themselves about the others'? (A)

3. What term was given to the policy whereby Britannia and Colonia kept apart from the others? (A)

4. What agreement signed in 1902 marked the end of Britannia keeping apart the other powers? (A)

5. Which country is represented by: (a) the seated girl, (b) the gentleman, (c) the elderly chaperone? (B)

6. What was the name of the colonial agreement signed in 1904 between the gentleman and the girl? What were its main terms? (B)

7. The word Morocco is on the sofa. Why was Morocco particularly important at this time? (B)

8. Where was a conference held to decide Morocco's future in 1906?

9. What were the results of this conference for Germany?

10. Which country is represented by: (a) the gentleman siding up to the girl, (b) the girl dressed in the kimono? (C)

11. What agreement had the couple in the background signed in 1902? (C)

12. What does France want Russia to do with England? (C)

13. What does Russia mean by 'if he wouldn't tread on my toes'? (C)

14. What had happened between France and Britain, for France to say 'He's improved immensely. I find him adorable!'? (C)

15. What agreement was signed between Britain and Russia in 1907? What were its main terms? What effect did this agreement have on the pattern of alliances in Europe?

16. What reasons does the German newspaper give for securing Morocco? (D)

17. Why was the Pan German League so upset at Germany being overlooked in talks over Morocco? (D)

18. Why did the German government see the Entente Cordiale as a defeat for German policy? (D)

19. Why did the Kaiser visit Tangiers?

20. *Talking point*: 'The Moroccan Crisis was one giant German blunder'. Do you agree? Provide reasons.

21. Which diagram in (E) represents the system of alliances in: (a) 1882, (b) 1887, (c) 1894, (d) 1907. You may need to refer back to pages 1-5 to refresh your memory on the early alliances.

22. Copy and label the diagrams in their correct order into your book.

23. *Talking point*: 'Once the Triple Alliance was formed, a Triple Entente was bound to follow'. Do you agree? Provide reasons.

24. After the Triple Entente was formed, the Germans complained of being encircled. Was this a fair complaint? Comment.

25. Write an essay of 250-300 words: How did the breakdown of the Bismarckian alliance system lead to the formation of new great power alignments by 1907?

4 – The Balkan Powderkeg

Europe's powder keg nearly explodes into war when Austria-Hungary annexes Bosnia and Herzegovina.

The Clash of Empires

The Balkans (South-East Europe) was known as the powder keg of Europe. One spark and the region seemed likely to explode into war.

Three empires — Turkey, Austria-Hungary, and Russia — were clashing in the Balkans.

The Turkish or Ottoman Empire had once ruled over all the Balkans. Known as the sick man of Europe, it was struggling to hold onto its remaining Balkan territories (see map). As the Turkish Empire had weakened, groups such as the Serbs, Greeks and Bulgars had revolted and set up their own separate nation states.

The Austro-Hungarian or Habsburg Empire was also a multi-national empire under nationalistic pressures from among its different racial groups. Under 50 percent of the empire's 50 million subject people belonged to the two privileged nationalities that controlled the empire — the German-speaking Austrians and the Magyars of Hungary. There were also 8.4 million Czechs and Slovaks, 5 million Poles, 4 million Ruthenians, 5.5 million Serbs, Croats and Solvenes and 770,000 Italians. Of the various groups, the south Slavs were the most restless and best organised. They wanted to break away from Austria-Hungary, and with the neighbouring kingdom of Serbia form one South Slav kingdom. Serbia was therefore seen by Austria as a threat to her continued survival. If Serbia was able to chip away at her empire then Austria-Hungary would disintegrate like Turkey.

The other empire with territorial designs in the Balkans was Russia. Much of Russia's trade passed from the Black Sea into the Mediterranean via the straits of Constantinople. Direct control or influence over the Balkans would protect this vital waterway. The Russians also sympathised with Serbs and the other Balkan nationalists. They shared the same Orthodox religion as most Balkan Slavs. Indeed Russia saw herself as champion of the Slav people.

The Bosnian Crisis

In 1908 a group of young radical officers seized power in Turkey. One of their aims was to rebuild the Turkish Empire. It seemed likely that they would try and reclaim the

Balkan provinces of Bosnia and Herzegovinia. These lands were part of the Turkish Empire but had been occupied by Austria since 1878.

To foil the Turks, the Austrians wanted to annex the two provinces. Russian support for such a plan was however essential. In September 1908, Aehrenthal, the Austrian Foreign Minister met in secret at Buchlau with his Russian counterpart Iswolsky. There the two ministers made a secret deal. In return for Russian approval of the annexation, Austria would support Russian moves to gain free access for its warships from the Black Sea to the Mediterranean through the straits at Constantinople. But the plan misfired. Before Iswolsky could secure British and French support for his side of the Buchlau bargain, Austria annexed Bosnia-Herzegovinia.

Iswolsky felt tricked. Moreover, when he returned home, his government, anxious to keep its good name among the Slavs, disowned his bargain and protested against the annexation.

Serbia appealed to Russia for help to fight Austria-Hungary. Russia however told Serbia to be patient and called for an international conference to investigate the annexation.

But Austria refused. Backed up by Germany who virtually threatened war unless Russia accepted the annexation, the Russians had to back down. With vastly inferior forces they were no match for the German war machine.

The Aftermath

Although war was averted, the price of the Austrian victory was high. Russia was embittered and began to rearm in earnest. Never again would she back down in such humiliating circumstances. Relations with Germany and Austria permanently soured. Serbia remained incensed and openly began to support terrorist liberation groups. War with Austria-Hungary seemed only a matter of time. In throwing her military might behind Austria, Germany revealed how desperate she was to retain the loyalty of her only reliable ally.

(A) A French cartoon on the Bosnian Crisis, 1908. Fat mama — Turkey — weeps helplessly while villain Austria steals her children in 1908.

(B)

AN IMAGINARY DISCUSSION AMONG SOME BOSNIANS

Ilić : We must free ourselves from Austrian rule. Only then will we be able to preserve our traditions, language and religion.

Popović : I agree. We could join up with our fellow Slavs in Serbia. I am sure Serbia would help us.

Grabež : That's easier said than done. Serbia is too weak to defeat Austria alone. Nevertheless there is always a chance that Russia will help her.

Obilić : I say be patient. It is only a matter of time until the Austrian Empire collapses. When that day comes we must be ready.

(C) THE BALKANS IN 1909

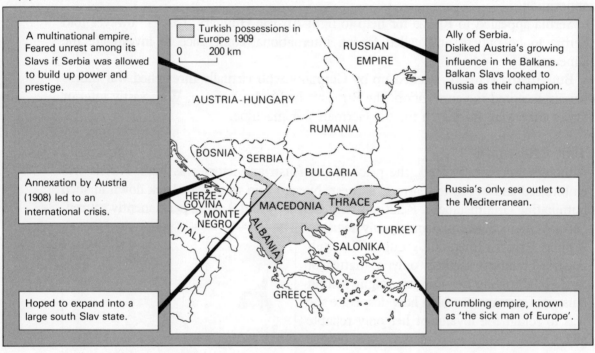

A multinational empire. Feared unrest among its Slavs if Serbia was allowed to build up power and prestige.

Ally of Serbia. Disliked Austria's growing influence in the Balkans. Balkan Slavs looked to Russia as their champion.

Annexation by Austria (1908) led to an international crisis.

Russia's only sea outlet to the Mediterranean.

Hoped to expand into a large south Slav state.

Crumbling empire, known as 'the sick man of Europe'.

Turkish possessions in Europe 1909

0   200 km

RUSSIAN EMPIRE

AUSTRIA-HUNGARY

RUMANIA

BOSNIA   SERBIA

BULGARIA

HERZE-GOVINA

MONTE NEGRO

MACEDONIA   THRACE

ITALY

ALBANIA

TURKEY

SALONIKA

GREECE

(D)

THE BLUNDERING KAISER:
THE DAILY TELEGRAPH INTERVIEW OF 1908
While the Bosnian Crisis was developing, an interview given by the Kaiser during his 1907 visit to England was published in the *Daily Telegraph*. The interview published on 28th October 1908 provoked a howl of indignation from English readers:

THE
GERMAN EMPEROR
AND
ENGLAND.

PERSONAL INTERVIEW.

FRANK STATEMENT
OF
WORLD POLICY.

(i)
'You English are mad, mad, mad as March Hares,' said the German monarch. 'What has come over you that you are so completely given over to suspicions quite unworthy of a great nation? What more can I do than I have done?

'I have declared with all the emphasis at my command . . . that my heart is set upon peace, and that it is one of my dearest wishes to live on the best terms with England. Have I ever been false to my word? Falsehood and prevarication are alien to my nature . . . (but) . . . your press, or at any rate a considerable portion of it, bids the people of England to refuse my proffered hand, insinuates that the other holds a dagger. How can I convince a nation against its will?'

The Kaiser then discussed Anglo-German relations during the Boer War:

'Just at the time of your Black Week, in December 1899, when disasters followed one another in rapid succession, I received a letter from Queen Victoria, my revered grandmother, written in sorrow and affliction, and bearing manifest traces of the anxieties which were preying on her mind and health. I at once returned a sympathetic reply. Nay I did more . . . I worked out what I considered to be the best plan of campaign under the circumstances, and submitted it to my general staff for their criticism. Then I despatched it to England, and that document . . . is among the state papers at Windsor Castle, awaiting the serenely impartial verdict of history.'

(ii)
After reading the *Daily Telegraph* interview Lord Esher wrote:

'He [the Kaiser] sits all Europe by the ears — or would if he could — in a rage of egoistic chatter . . . He fails to see that he could have furnished us with no more telling argument for 'keeping our powder dry'. A feckless man.'

ACTIVITIES

1. Who are represented by the two children? (A)

2. Why is Turkey portrayed as a fat mama? (A)

3. What political term is used to describe Austria's action? (A)

4. Why did Austria 'steal Turkey's children'? (A)

5. Which Balkan state was especially upset at Austria's action? Why? (A)

6. What role did Russia play in this whole affair?

7. How did Germany come to be involved in the Bosnian Crisis?

8. Quote from (B) the statement which gives the basis for nationalism.

9. Why did Ilić want Serbia to break away from Austrian control? (B)

10. Why did Popović want to join up with Serbia? (B)

11. Copy map (C) into your book. To understand this topic you will need to be familiar with all the places on the map, so learn it off by heart.

12. *Talking point:* Imagine Russia did help Serbia fight Austria like Grabez was hoping for. Which power would have come to Austria's aid? Why? How could this have led to a European war?

13. *Talking point:* Austria-Hungary was once described as 'a broken pot held together by a piece of wire'. What is meant by this statement?

14. What impression does the interview leave of the Kaiser's attitude towards the English? (D)

15. Why was it tactless for the Kaiser to revive memories of the Boer War? (D)

16. Who did the Kaiser claim gave the tactical advice which helped the British overcome their Boer War disasters? (D)

17. The Kaiser's intention with the interview was to reassure the English that 'his heart was set on peace'. What comment of Lord Esher's suggests the interview had the opposite effect? (D)

18. The Kaiser had a reputation as 'le plus grand gaffeur de L'Europe' (the greatest blunderer in Europe). After reading the *Daily Telegraph* interview, do you think this title was justified?

5 – The Arms Race

An arms race develops as the European powers increase their arms spending. The launching of the HMS Dreadnought *turn British-German naval rivalry into a full scale naval race.*

The Naval Race

At first the British ignored the German naval buildup, but the Second Naval Law of 1900 opened their eyes. This called for doubling the German battleship fleet by 1916. The threat of Germany as a major naval power as well as the strongest land power in Europe suddenly loomed.

The challenge was taken up in earnest in 1903 when the British Parliament approved the formation of a North Sea fleet based at the new naval base at Rosyth. In 1906, under the guidance of the dynamic new First Sea Lord, Sir John Fisher, the British navy launched a battleship which rendered all existing battleships obsolete. HMS *Dreadnought* as it was called could outgun and outrace any battleship afloat. Not surprisingly the Germans were horrified. Rumours circulated that the British might launch a surprise raid on the German fleet. To a certain extent, these fears were fuelled by the Anglo-Russian Entente of 1907. With Britain allied to both France and Russia in the Triple Entente, the Germans felt they were being encircled by a coalition of hostile powers.

Yet if the *Dreadnought* revealed the shortcomings of the German fleet, it also made most British battleships obsolete. By building 'Dreadnoughts' of their own, the Germans could quickly cut back the British naval lead. So, Germany began to build its own fleet of 'Dreadnoughts'. Britain replied by speeding up her own shipbuilding programme. A full scale naval race had begun.

Military Spending Increases

The naval race was part of a general arms race. Between 1870 and 1914 military spending by the European powers multiplied 300 percent. Increases in population made man-power available for huge standing armies, and following the German example, conscription was adopted by all the continental powers after 1871.

The chief feature of the arms race on land was the contest for numerical supremacy. Germany set the pace: in 1874 she had a peacetime army of 400,000; by 1914 it had risen to 800,000. In wartime she could field 5,600,000 trained troops, in a real emergency

8,500,000 could be called to the colours. France, with its much lower population kept up by training every available man. On mobilisation in 1914, France could field 3,500,000 soldiers. Russia, with its huge population, trained a smaller percentage of eligible males. Even so, it still had a peace strength of 1,430,000 and some 5,000,000 trained for war.

(A)

1872-1912   SPENDING ON ARMAMENTS

PERCENTAGE INCREASE

(chart showing percentage increase for GERMANY, RUSSIA, ITALY, ENGLAND, AUSTRIA/HUNGARY, FRANCE)

(D)
HMS *Dreadnought* (1906) 17,900 tons. Length: 526 ft. Ten 12 in. guns. Five torpedo tubes. Armour: 11 in. Top speed: 21.6 knots.

(B)

GERMANY

Date	Size of army	Size of navy	Total	% of population
1880	401,650	7,350	409,000	0.9
1891	511,650	17,000	528,650	1.07
1901	604,100	31,200	635,300	1.16
1911	622,500	33,500	656,000	1.01
1914	791,000	73,000	864,000	1.3

GREAT BRITAIN

Date	Size of army	Size of navy	Total	% of population
1880	198,200	59,000	257,200	0.73
1891	209,000	97,600	306,600	0.8
1901	773,500	114,900	888,400	2.1 (Boer War)
1911	247,000	128,000	375,000	0.83
1914	247,000	146,000	393,000	0.85

Proportion of population in the armed forces 1880-1914
(from *The Kaiser and His Times* by M. Balfour)

(C)
Pre-Dreadnought battleship: HMS *Dominion* (built 1905) 16,350 tons.
Length: 457 ft. Four 12 in. guns. Four 9 in. guns. Five torpedo tubes.
Armour: 9 in. Top speed: 18.2 knots.

THE NAVAL RACE

Date	German Naval Expansion	British Naval Expansion
1898	First Naval Act: 19 battleships to be built by 1905.	
1900	Second Naval Act: number of battleships to be doubled by 1916.	
1902		German building plans arouse concern of British press.
1903		New naval base at Rosyth built. Plans approved for formation of a North Sea fleet.
1906 (Feb)		HMS *Dreadnought* is launched. Can outgun and outrace any battleship afloat.
1906 (May)	Tonnage of ships under construction increased, six cruisers added to the building programme. Plans approved for widening of Kiel Canal to take 'Dreadnoughts'.	
1908	Naval Act amended: four 'Dreadnoughts' to be built each year up to 1911 instead of three.	
1909		Alarm at speed of German naval construction. Britain announces the building of eight 'Dreadnoughts' instead of three.
1912	New Naval Law further expands fleet.	Naval convention strengthens Franco-Russian entente. Anglo-French Naval Convention. Britain agrees to police North Sea, while France looks after the Mediterranean.
Date	German Naval Expansion	British Naval Expansion
1914		Informal talks between British and Russian naval officials. According to Winston Churchill naval rivalry between Britain and Germany had ceased to be a source of friction, because 'it was certain that we (Britain) could not be overtaken as far as capital ships were concerned'. (W.S. Churchill, *The World Crisis, 1911-1914*)

(F)

THE NAVAL SCARE OF 1909

In the spring of 1909 there was a false scare that Germany was secretly building battleships.

To maintain superiority over the suspected German building, the Admiralty demanded that six new battleships be built. The Liberal Party opposed this and said four new ships would be adequate. But Navalists and Conservatives went beyond Admiralty's proposal and demanded eight. A conservative MP coined a phrase which soon became a national slogan: *"We want eight and we won't wait."*

The *Observer* (21 March) advised Englishmen to:

'Insist on the Eight the whole Eight, and nothing but the Eight, with more to follow, with more to follow, and break any man or faction that stands in the way'.

(G)

THE NAVAL RACE		
Dreadnoughts	Great Britain	Germany
1906	1	—
1907	3	—
1908	2	4
1909	2	3
1910	3	1
1911	5	3
1912	3	2
1913	7	3
1914	3	1
total:	29	17
Dreadnought Battle-cruisers		
1906	—	—
1907	3	—
1908	—	—
1909	1	—
1910	1	2
1911	2	1
1912	1	2
1913	1	2
1914	—	—
total:	9	7

(H) THE MARINE PAINTERS OF ENGLAND AND GERMANY
Uncle Edward (to William): 'Your little marine masterpiece is too ambitious; keep it as a study.'

ACTIVITIES

1. What was the average percentage increase in arms spending between 1872 and 1912? (A)

2. Which country had the highest percentage increase? (A)

3. Compare the British and German armed forces between 1880 and 1914. What changes took place over this period? (B)

4. List three ways in which HMS *Dreadnought* was a superior fighting ship to HMS *Dominion*. (C) (D)

5. How did the launching of the *Dreadnought* in 1906 accelerate the naval race between Britain and Germany?

6. Make a note of the key dates in the naval race. (E)

7. What was the naval scare of 1909? What effect did it have on the naval race? (F)

8. Why were some groups in Britain and Germany only too happy to encourage false rumours about each other's navies?

9. Who won the naval race between 1906 and 1914? Quote figures. (G)

10. According to Churchill what was the state of the naval race on the eve of the First World War? (F)

11. Identify the two marine painters? How are they portrayed? (H)

12. What did Uncle Edward mean by 'your marine masterpiece is too ambitious'? (H)

13. With whom do the cartoonist's sympathy's seem to lie? Give reasons? (H)

14. *Talking point:* 'The way the British reacted to the German naval challenge was plain arrogance. If it was good enough for the British to have a huge navy it was good enough for the Germans.' Do you agree? Provide reasons.

15. *Talking point:* 'A strong defence force is the best way to keep peace.' Discuss.

6 – The Will to Make War

European society accepts war as natural and inevitable.

Literature

In the popular pre-First World War literature, war novels were often best sellers. War was treated as normal and romantic. War was presented as a quick and attractive way of settling international disputes. Victories were always total and decisive — resulting in peace and future happiness.

While novels can be dismissed as lighthearted escapism, non-fiction works must be treated more seriously. In Germany General Bernhardi's book *Germany and the New War* published in 1912 quickly reached six editions. For General Bernhardi the alternatives for Germany were either as a 'world power or destruction'.

The Press

The end of the nineteenth century saw the rise of mass literacy accompanied by a mass-circulation press. Newspaper proprietors quickly learnt that bad news sold more papers than good. Minor incidents were blown up into major crises. Too often newspapers inflamed nationalistic feelings by playing on national hatreds.

Patriotic Education

In the late nineteenth century education became much more widely available throughout Europe. Rich and poor were now taught about their past. From their earliest days, the French were taught how the murdering Germans had robbed them of their two children, Alsace and Lorraine. In German schools, children were taught how poor Germany was surrounded by enemies. Russians learned of the numerous invasions they had suffered throughout their history.

The most famous of all the imaginary war novels was William Le Queux's *Invasion of 1910*. First serialised by the *Daily Mail* in 1906, it later sold over a million copies as a book.

At the top of the next page is an extract taken from the book:

(A)

(B)

In a series of reports on Germany, the British mass circulation *Daily Mail* in 1909 proclaimed:

'Germany is deliberately preparing to destroy the British Empire . . . All Europe is to be Teutonised. We are all to be drilled and schooled and uniformed and taxed by Prussian officials and the Emperor William II is to rule us with a rod of iron . . . Britain alone stands in the way of Germany's realisation of world-power and domination.'

(C)

WAR

IS A PART

OF

GOD'S

ETERNAL PLAN

Hellmult von Moltke, 1880

One of a number of famous sayings used by a German cigarette manufacturer in his advertisements.

(D) General Baden Powell talking to a group of Boy Scouts, 1908.

ACTIVITIES

1. Compare the extracts from William Le Quex's novel and the *Daily Mail*. Who is portrayed as the enemy? (A) (B)

2. Which one was likely to have been the more damaging to international goodwill?

3. Was it responsible journalism for the *Daily Mail* to run its series of reports on Germany? Comment.

4. What does the fact that German manufacturers used sayings such as (C) in their advertisements tell us about popular attitudes in Germany? (C)

5. *Talking point:* Who do novels today portray as the enemy we must most fear? Should novels which play on national hatreds be banned in the cause of world peace?

6. What do the uniforms of the Scouts suggest they were influenced by?

7. The Boy Scouts founded in 1908 by General Baden Powell was designed to provide the soldiers of the future; the Boys Brigade and the Territorials were also founded at this time. How could such organisations help train children for war so that they regarded war as natural and inevitable?

8. Do the Scouts and Boys Brigade perform a similar function today?

9. *Talking point:* Is it right for schools to teach patriotism? Is patriotism a good thing?

7 – The Agadir Incident 1911

German gunboat diplomacy sparks off the second Moroccan Crisis.

Ever since the Algeciras conference of 1906, the situation in Morocco had remained unstable. Early in 1911 the Sultan of Morocco called for French help to crush a revolt by rebel tribesmen.

Gunboat Diplomacy

Germany was certain this would be followed by a French takeover. So as soon as the French occupied the capital, Fez, Germany sent the gunboat *Panther* to the Moroccan port of Agadir. This gunboat diplomacy was followed by a German demand for compensation. In exchange for the whole of the French Congo in Central Africa, Germany would let France have Morocco.

British Reaction

The move, however, badly misfired and alarmed the British. The Kaiser, they thought (wrongly as it turned out) meant to turn Agadir into a German naval base close to Gibraltar and vital British trade routes. And here it seemed was yet another crude German attempt to destroy the Anglo-French entente.

Lloyd George, the British Chancellor of the Exchequer warned Germany that Britain would fight rather than see herself or her allies pushed around in this way. Britain's fleet was even prepared for war. In the end Germany climbed down and accepted two strips of territory in the French Congo — a far smaller area than it had originally demanded.

Results of the Crisis

Yet the damage had been done. Britain was more than ever convinced Germany wanted to dominate Europe. For the Germans, the result was another humiliating diplomatic defeat. Nor could they forget Lloyd George's fighting speech. Here it seemed was further proof that Germany was being encircled by a ring of vicious enemies. Tirpitz used the crisis to push through another naval law to further expand the German navy. Britain followed suit. As a result, Britain and France drew closer together. In the Anglo-French Naval Convention of 1912 Britain agreed to police the North Sea while France looked after the Mediterranean. The Anglo-French entente was now virtually a military alliance.

(A)

THE MAILED FIST OF AGADIR
A German cartoon.

(B)   **SOLID**
Germany: 'Donnerwetter! It's rock. I thought it was going to be paper.'

A British cartoon on the Agadir incident

(C)

(i) During the Moroccan crisis von Moltke, the German Chief of General Staff wrote to his wife:

'I am thoroughly fed up with this wretched Morocco affair . . . If once again we crawl out of this affair with our tail between our legs, if we cannot pluck up the courage to take a [tough] line which we are prepared to enforce with the sword then I despair of the future of the German empire. Than I shall quit. But before that I shall propose that we do away with the army and place ourselves under the protection of Japan; then we can concentrate on making money and become country bumpkins.'

(ii) At the height of the Agadir Crisis, Lloyd George made use of a speech to London bankers at the Mansion House to deliver a clear warning:

'I would make great sacrifices to preserve peace. I conceive that nothing would justify a disturbance of international goodwill except questions of the gravest national moment. But if a situation were to be forced upon us in which peace could only be preserved . . . by allowing Britain to be treated, where her interests were vitally affected, as if she were of no account in the Cabinet of Nations, then I say emphatically that peace at that price would be a humiliation intolerable for a great country like ours to endure.'

(iii) Eventually the Germans climbed down, but a feeling of bitterness remained. In the Reichstag the Conservative leader was applauded with his reply to Lloyd George.

'When we hear a speech that we must consider as a threat, as a challenge, as a humiliating challenge, it is not so easy to pass it over as after-dinner speechifying. Such incidents like a flash in the dark show the German peoples where is the foe. The German people now knows, when it seeks foreign expansion, such as is its right and destiny, where it has to look for permission. We Germans are not accustomed to that and cannot allow it and we shall know how to answer.'

ACTIVITIES

1. Whose mailed fist is shown? (A)

2. Why is the phrase 'gunboat diplomacy' appropriate to the Agadir incident? (A)

3. What comment is the cartoonist making about Germany's handling of the Agadir crisis? (A)

4. What does the British cartoon suggest was behind Germany's actions over Morocco in 1911? (B)

5. What point about the Entente Cordiale is the cartoon making? (B)

6. In your opinion is the cartoon an accurate comment on the effects of the Agadir incident? (B)

7. Why was Moltke so annoyed by the Moroccan affair? (C)

8. What warning did Lloyd George deliver to Germany in his Mansion House address? (C)

9. How did the German Conservative leader react to the speech? (C)

10. Why did he feel that Germany was entitled to expand into areas like Morocco? (C)

38

8 – War Clouds Over the Balkans

Serbia emerges from the Balkan Wars as the largest and most powerful of the Balkan nations.

In 1912, encouraged by the Russians, the Balkan States of Serbia, Greece, Bulgaria and Montenegro put aside their quarrels to form an alliance called the Balkan League.

The First Balkan War

In October 1912, the armies of the League took advantage of their newly combined strength to attack their hated neighbour, Turkey. Already weakened by a war with Italy the year before, the Turks were in seven weeks almost completely driven out of Europe. Austria, watching on, was stunned. Five centuries of Turkish rule in Europe had suddenly ended. Worse still, Serbia had come out as the strongest Balkan state. What was Austria to do? The Austrian generals called for a quick war to crush Serbia once and for all. But if Austria attacked Serbia, Russia would back the Serbs. If Russia attacked Austria, Germany would back the Austrians. If the Germans attacked Russia, France would be drawn in. Finally, if France was attacked, Britain might be drawn in. In other words the system of alliances meant an attack on Serbia could trigger off a European war. And in 1912, none of the great powers — including Austria — wanted that.

So the great powers stepped in and forced a peace settlement on the Balkan states. At the peace conference, Austria thwarted Serbia's plans for a coastline by having a new country, Albania, placed between Serbia and the Adriatic Sea (see map B). The rest of the conquered Turkish lands were shared out among the Balkan League.

The Second Balkan War

But within a month the Balkan League had fallen out over the spoils. Bulgaria quarrelled with Serbia and Greece. In June 1913 the Bulgarians began the second Balkan War by attacking their former allies. They were, however, quickly defeated. In the peace settlement that followed Bulgaria surrendered nearly all the lands she had won in the first war to Greece and Serbia.

The Legacy of the Balkan Wars

The Balkan Wars had a disastrous effect on Austro-Serbian relations. Serbia felt cheated at being cut off from the sea by Albania. The Serbian press became ever more virulent in its demands for slavic unity. Serb terrorist attacks against Austrian targets were openly applauded. For her part, Austria resented Serbia's recent successes. The Balkan Wars had seen Serbia double in size and turn into a formidable military power. Urgent and drastic action was called for. It was now only a matter of waiting for the right opportunity.

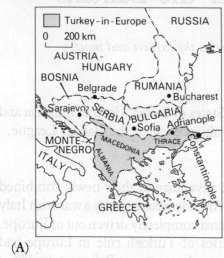

(A)
The Balkans in 1912 before the Balkan Wars.

(B)
The Balkans in 1913 after the Balkan Wars.

ACTIVITIES

1. Compare the two maps of the Balkans before and after the Balkan Wars. Which empire lost most of its European territory? (A) (B)

2. Which country expanded its territory the most? (A) (B)

3. How and why was a new country created on Serbia's western border?

4. Explain how a) Austria and b) Serbia felt about the changed map of the Balkans in 1913?

5. The 'successes of the Balkan League represented a tremendous triumph for Russian policy and were a stunning blow to Germany and Austria' — L.C.F. Turner. In what sense was this true?

6. Why did the Balkan League and Turkey go to war in 1912 and 1913? (C)

7. Why is the war between the Balkan League and Turkey portrayed as a vortex or whirlpool? (C)

8. Why is peace shown as struggling to hold onto the great powers? (C)

9. Identify the countries sitting on the boiling cauldron? (D)

10. What were the Balkan troubles which brought the cauldron to boiling point? (D)

11. What would happen if the cauldron boiled over? (D)

12. Compare the two cartoons on the Balkans in 1912. What general point are they making? (C) (D)

(C)   THE VORTEX
Will the powers be drawn in? A fantasy by David Wilson.
(*Punch*, 1912)

The Balkan League states fight Turkey in the First Balkan War while the
Great Powers look on.

(D) THE BOILING POINT
(*Punch*, 2 October 1912)

9 – Planning for Victory

The European Powers prepare detailed mobilisation plans. In particular, Germany's Schlieffen plan is extraordinarily risky and dangerous.

In the years before World War I every European power made elaborate plans on what to do if war broke out. Drawn up by the military experts, the generals and admirals, these plans were necessarily very detailed. Conscripts had to be called up to be organised into fighting units. Troops had to be provided with arms, clothing, food and other equipment. Then they had to be transported to the battle front as quickly as possible.

Mobilisation

Readying an army for war is called mobilisation. Rapid mobilisation was widely regarded as essential for a quick victory. The army which mobilised first, could strike and might evem win the war before the other side was ready. The key to high speed mobilisation was the railway. Only the railway could transport large armies at high speed to the battle front. Every general was aware that Prussia's decisive victories over Austria and France in 1866 and 1870 were underpinned by the best railroad networks in Europe.

The railways had one enormous disadvantage; they were extraordinarily rigid. Once a plan was set in motion it was virtually impossible to change without throwing the rest of the timetable into chaos. Any delay of course would give the enemy a vital head start.

The Schlieffen Plan

The German war plan was named after its designer, Count Von Schlieffen. The Germans believed that war with France was inevitable. The French wanted revenge for their defeat by Germany in 1870-71. As France was allied to Russia any future war would therefore be a two-front war with both France and Russia.

But Schlieffen believed that the German army was not strong enough to fight both sides at the same time. What could be done? Schlieffen's answer was simple. Knowing that the Russian armies would take six weeks to mobilise, Schlieffen worked out a plan based on crushing France first. By making maximum use of the railways, he calculated, that in six weeks the German armies could knock out France and still have time to move to the Eastern Front to face the Russian armies who would still be organising.

But the plan had two giant flaws. Firstly, there was no plan for a war with only Russia. Incredibly, a war with Russia meant Germany had to first attack France. Secondly, to defeat France quickly, Germany had to avoid the heavily fortified French-German border. To get around the French forts, Germany planned to invade France through Belgium and catch the French by surprise. Belgium was a neutral country and her right to stay neutral was guaranteed by a treaty signed by Britain. By planning to invade France through Belgium, Germany was risking a war with Britain.

> " BELGIUM .... SHALL FORM AN INDEPENDENT AND PERPETUALLY NEUTRAL STATE. IT SHALL BE BOUND TO OBSERVE SUCH NEUTRALITY TOWARDS ALL OTHER STATES."

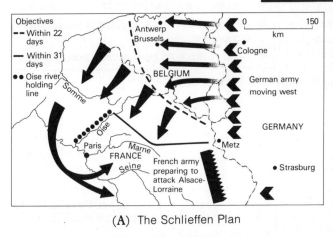

(A) The Schlieffen Plan

These are the Seals and Signatures of the Six Nations who guaranteed Belgian Independence and Neutrality

GREAT BRITAIN - Palmerston
BELGIUM - Sylvain Van De Weyer
AUSTRIA - Senfft
FRANCE - H. Sebastiani
GERMANY - Bülow
RUSSIA - Pozzo Di Borgo

(B) Part of a British poster illustrating the Treaty of London 1839, guaranteeing Belgium's neutrality.

(C)

WAR BY TIMETABLE

'All the great powers had vast conscript armies [armies of civilians who had been trained to fight and who were kept in reserve]. These armies of course were not maintained in peace time. They were brought together by mobilisation. . . . All mobilisation plans depended on the railways. At that time the automobile was hardly used, and railways demand timetables.

All the mobilisation plans had been timed to the minute, months or even years before and they could not be changed. [A change] in one direction would ruin them in every other direction. Any attempt for instance by the Austrians to mobilise against Serbia would mean that they could not then mobilise as well against Russia because two lots of trains would be running against each other . . . Any alteration in the mobilisation plan meant not a delay for 24 hours but for at least six months before the next lot of timetables were ready.'

(A.J.P. Taylor, *How Wars Begin*)

(D)

TO MOBILISE OR PREPARE AN ARMY FOR WAR WAS A HUGE JOB. HERE IS A DESCRIPTION OF WHAT MOBILISATION MEANT FOR THE GERMAN ARMY.

'Once the mobilisation button was pushed the whole vast machinery for calling up, equipping and transporting two million men began turning automatically. Reservists went to designated depots, were issued uniforms, equipment and arms, formed into companies and companies into battalions, were joined by cavalry, cyclists, artillery, medical units, cook-wagons, blacksmith wagons, even postal wagons, moved according to prepared railway timetables to concentration points near the frontier where they would be formed into divisions, divisions into corps and corps into armies ready to advance and fight. One army corps alone — out of the total of forty in the German forces — required 170 railway carriages for officers, 965 for infantry, 2960 for cavalry, 1915 for artillery and supply wagons — 6010 in all — grouped in 140 trains, and an equal number again for their supplies.'

(B. Tuchman, *August 1914*)

(E)

THE LESSONS OF 1905

The land battles of the Russo-Japanese war of 1904-05 were the largest seen for decades. Observers from the Great Powers flocked to the battlefields of Manchuria to observe the war.

Yet few important lessons were learnt from the battles which foreshadowed the First World War.

Among the lessons to be learnt were:

● Trenches, machine guns and barbwire could stop the most determined of enemies

● Trench warfare meant battles were long, indecisive with enormous casualties

● Frontal attacks had little effect on the enemy

● Modern artillery was capable of tremendous devastation

● Against machine guns cavalry was useless

ACTIVITIES

1. Why didn't the German armies attack France across the French-German frontier? (A)

2. Describe how the German armies planned to defeat the French forces. (A)

3. Do you think it was wrong for Germany to invade France through Belgium? Provide reasons. (B)

4. Why was it so difficult for the Great Powers to change their war plans at the last moment? (C)

5. Suggest why the generals had to plan their mobilisation in great detail. (D)

6. What lessons did the Great Powers fail to learn from the Russo-Japanese War? (E)

7. If the generals had forseen the horrors of World War I, do you think they would have been more careful and urged their political masters to be more cautious?

8. *Talking point:* Imagine you were in command of the German army. Mobilisation had begun as in (D) and your troops are moving by railway towards the French frontier. At the last moment the Emperor orders you to stop the attack on France and attack Russia instead. What problems would you face?

10 – The Final Crisis

The assassination of the Austrian heir triggers off another
Balkan Crisis. Russia and Germany mobilise their armies
making European war inevitable.

In early 1914 all the European powers stepped up their armaments programmes. Nevertheless relations between Britain and Germany were exceptionally calm. In June a Royal Navy squadron even paid a goodwill visit to Germany.

Assassination at Sarajevo

On 28 June, the Archduke Ferdinand, heir to the Austrian throne was assassinated in Sarajevo, the capital of Bosnia.

The assassination was the work of a group of young Bosnian terrorists dedicated to the cause of a Greater Serbia. The group had been armed by the 'Black Hand' — a Serbian secret society headed by Colonel Dragutin Dimitrijevic who was also Serbia's Chief of Army intelligence. In fact the plot was known to Serbia's Prime Minister, Nikola Pasic, who sent a vague warning to Vienna urging the Archduke to cancel his visit to Sarajevo.

The assassination very nearly failed. In a first attempt on the morning of 28 June, the bomb fell on the folded roof of the open car and bounced back into the street behind. With that the plot appeared to have failed. But incredibly, that afternoon, the Archduke drove out on the open streets again. One of the conspirators, Gavrilo Princip spotted the Archduke's car opposite him. Seizing his chance, Princip stepped forward, withdrew his revolver and fired two shots killing the Archduke and his wife.

Austria Reacts

The Austrian government was enraged at the assassination. Although there was no clear proof, nobody doubted that Serbia was behind what had happened. The time had come to crush Serbia once and for all.

A war with Serbia presented two main obstacles; first the Austrian army needed a month to prepare for war and second, would Germany back Austria if Russia came to Serbia's aid?

At a meeting in Berlin on 5 July, the Kaiser supported by his Chancellor Bethmann-Hollwegg, threw his full weight behind the Austrian plan. Germany was ready to march if Russian armies moved in support of Austria.

By giving Austria a free hand to invade Serbia, the Germans knew they were risking a European war. Nevertheless, failure to back Austria might result in Germany losing its last powerful ally. The Kaiser it seems did not think the Russians would back the Serbians. More important, the German army did not think the Russians were ready for war. Russia's war plans were still incomplete. The country still seemed to be recovering from its disastrous war with Japan in 1905. If there was to be a war with Russia and France as well, now was better than later.

Ultimatum to Serbia

On 23 July the Austrians presented Serbia one of the harshest ultimatums ever delivered in diplomatic history. Included were demands which no self-respecting nation could possibly accept. Moreover, unconditional acceptance was required within 48 hours.

Serbia accepted virtually all of the demands but even this didn't satisfy Austria. Their minds were set on war.

In the meantime, the British Prime Minister, Sir Edward Grey called for a four power conference between the great powers to resolve the dispute. But the Germans refused to take part. They still thought they could keep the dispute localised in the Balkans. They were wrong. Thus on 28 July Austria declared war on Serbia. The next day Austrian shells bombarded Belgrade.

Russia Intervenes

On 30 July the Tsar ordered Russia's armies to mobilise. Encouraged by French assurances, Russian military preparations had begun in secret five days before.

This time the Russians were determined to back Serbia to the hilt. There would be no humiliating backdown such as there had been over Bosnia in 1908-09. Russia's decision to mobilise accelerated the pace of events and cut the time available for negotiations to virtually nil.

Germany Mobilises

The rigid dictates of the Schieffen Plan meant Germany had to counter with immediate mobilisation. Mobilisation for the German army meant war. Eleven thousand trains carrying troops, arms and supplies were now to be despatched to the French frontier via Belgium. If Belgium objected, then plans for an immediate invasion would be actioned. Time was critical. Any hold up over Belgium would create havoc with the railway timetables. There was only six weeks to knock out France. Any longer and the Russians would have the time they needed to mobilise and attack Germany. If that happened, Germany would face war on two fronts and years of planning would have been wasted.

On 31 July Germany issued two ultimatums; the first gave the Russians 12 hours to demobilise, the second gave the French 18 hours to promise their neutrality if a Russo-German war broke out.

War (August 1-4)

When the ultimatum to Russia expired on 1 August, Germany declared war and began to mobilise. That same day the French after rejecting Germany's ultimatum also ordered general mobilisation.

On 2 August, the Germans invaded Luxembourg and presented an ultimatum to the Belgiums demanding the right to send troops through their country.

Any attack on Belgium was likely to draw Britain into the war. As a signatory to the 1839 Treaty of London, Britain was bound to protect Belgium's neutrality. There were of course also Britain's treaty and military ties with France and Russia. The preservation of France was essential to Britain's national interest. It was doubtful if Britain could afford to let Germany dominate Continental Europe. If there was going to be a showdown over European supremacy it seemed better to fight before Germany became all powerful.

On Monday 3 August, Belgium rejected Germany's ultimatum and appealed to the signatories of the 1839 treaty for help. That same day German troops crossed into Belgium.

On Tuesday 4 August, the British sent an ultimatum to Berlin. Unless Germany called off her invasion of Belgium within five hours, the British would sever diplomatic relations. At midnight on 4 August, the ultimatum expired and Great Britain declared war on Germany.

In just five weeks a Balkan dispute had escalated into a European war. Eventually nations from every part of the globe would become involved. The First Word War had begun.

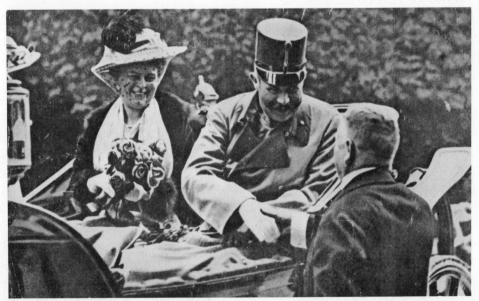

(A) The Archduke and his wife about to drive away from the Town Hall — not long before the assassination.

HE WONT BE
HAPPY TILL HE
GETS IT

EUROPE

(C) British postcard of 1914.

(E)

HOW THE SCHLIEFFEN PLAN PUSHED EUROPE INTO WAR

'One essential part of the [Schlieffen] plan was to go through Belgium. The other essential part which was equally important was that there could be no delay between mobilisation and war because if there were delay then Russia would catch up and the Germans would get the two-front war after all. So the moment that the Germans decided on mobilisation, they decided for war, or rather war followed of itself. The railway timetables . . . in the Schlieffen Plan . . . brought the troops not to their barracks but into Belgium and Northern France. The German mobilisation plan actually laid down the first 40 days of the German invasion of France and none of it could be altered because if it did all the timetables would go wrong. Thus the decision for mobilisation which the Germans (announced on 1 August) was a decision for a general European war.'

A.J.P. Taylor (*How Wars Begin*)

(D) German cartoon. In the garden, a German waters his plants while an aggressive neighbour waves a stick.

(B)   BRAVO, BELGIUM!
How the British magazine *Punch* saw the outbreak of war.

(F)

The German mobilisation order was signed at 5 o'clock in the afternoon of Saturday 1 August. Soon afterwards, Bethmann-Hollwegg, the Chancellor and Jagow, Secretary of State for Foreign Affairs arrived with sensational news from London; a telegram from London from Lichnowsky (the German Ambassador to Britain), reporting that the British government promised France would remain neutral under a British guarantee. It seemed there was no need to attack France.

. . .'That calls for champagne!' cried the Kaiser, clapping his hands with delight. Turning to the Chief of Staff he said, 'We must provisionally halt the march towards the West.'

Moltke's colour, never good, changed for the worse. At this late hour the . . . timetable of mobilisation could not be altered, without some unimaginable chaos overtaking the whole exquisite schedule. Eleven thousand trains, waving to and fro over Germany's railway system in a closely timed and sinister ballet, would in a matter of hours call into being an army of 4,000,000 well-trained, superbly equipped and tensely organised soldiers launched on a supreme design: to reach Paris in 40 days! Already the trains were steaming into the sidings, the barracks were being made ready; the uniforms and the weapons were being laid out; already — General Helmuth von Moltke could hardly speak for emotion: 'That we can't do! The whole army would be thrown into confusion. We should lose any chance of victory.'

'Your uncle would not have given me that answer,' said the Kaiser reproachfully. He ordered a call to be put through to Trèves where the German advance guard was preparing to move into neutral Luxembourg.

Losing control of himself Moltke shouted, 'If I cannot march against France I cannot take responsibility for the war!' He stood trembling and mottled, as if he had suffered some seizure. Tears ran down his cheeks.

'And I,' cried Bethmann-Hollwegg, with equal emotion, 'can't take responsibility for failing to examine the British note!'

Bethmann and Jagow were told to . . . draft a reply to London. The Kaiser . . . wrote out a telegram to cousin Georgie: 'If Britain guarantees the neutrality of France I will abandon all action against her.'

Moltke, still shaking, still distraught, telephoned to the red brick building of the General Staff to stop the advance of the Sixteenth Division into Luxembourg — if it could be stopped. The general was not wholly successful. At seven o'clock, just half a company of German troops crossed the frontier of Luxembourg and destroyed the telephone and telegraph equipment at the railway station of Trois Vièrges. Half an hour later another party arrived and ordered the first party off: there had been a mistake . . .

In the early hours of the morning the Kaiser was awakened by his valet Schulz with the news that his aide-de-camp, Colonel von Mutius, sought an audience. Wearing a military greatcoat over his underclothes, the Kaiser read the telegram which Mutius brought. Georgie in London explained that Lichnowsky had got things wrong. Britain would guarantee the French neutrality only if Germany were neutral towards Russia as well as France.

The Kaiser called his Chief of the General Staff to the palace: 'Now you can do as you wish. March into Luxembourg.'

Moltke's agony was over.

(G.M. Thomson *The Twelve Days*)

COUNTDOWN TO WAR

1914	Austria-Hungary	Germany	Great Britain	Russia	France
June 28	Assassination of Austrian heir Franz Ferdinand.				
July 5		Kaiser assures Austrian ambassador of German support to crush Serbia.			
July 23	Austria delivers ultimatum to Serbia.				
July 26			Sir Edward Grey calls for a four-power conference.		
July 28	Austria declares war on Serbia.				
July 30				Russia mobilises.	
July 31		German ultimatum gives Russia 12 hours to demobilise.			
August 1		German ultimatum to Russia expires, Germany declares war on Russia and mobilises.			France mobilises.
August 2		Germany invades Luxembourg and sends an ultimatum to Belgium.			
August 3		Germany declares war on France, invades Belgium.	Britain mobilises army.		
August 4			British send ultimatum to Germany — ultimatum expires at midnight and Britain declares war on Germany.		

(H)

STAGES OF WAR	
Stage 1	Local War: (Austria vs. Serbia) — July 28
Stage 2	Continental War: Austria and Germany — August 1-3 vs. Russia and France
Stage 3	World War: Britain declares war — August 4

ACTIVITIES

1. Why would the Archduke and his wife have made an easy target for an assassin? (A)

2. Why is Germany threatening Belgium with a stick at the gate? (B)

3. Why does Germany want to get through the gate? (B)

4. With whom does the cartoonist sympathise? (B)

5. Explain how Belgium's refusal to let Germany through the gate brought Britain into the war?

6. Who is represented by the man in the bath? (C)

7. What does the British cartoon suggest caused World War I? (C)

8. How is Germany portrayed in cartoon (D)?

9. Identify Germany's two neighbours. (D)

10. Which neighbour in particular is portrayed as aggressive? (D)

11. Explain why A.J.P. Taylor's belief that the German decision to mobilise was bound to lead to a general European war (E) Do you agree?

12. Why was the Kaiser so jubilant on hearing the news from London? (F)

13. What did he want Moltke to do? Why was Moltke so upset? (F)

14. The Kaiser was often portrayed by his foreign neighbours as a warmonger. Was this a fair portrayal? (F)

15. *Talking point:* Study the timetable 'Countdown to War', along with the diagram showing the stages of war. Was their any stage where a European war might have been prevented? (G) (H)

11 – German Leadership and the July Crisis

Germany played a key role in the final crisis that led to the outbreak of World War I. In this unit we will examine some of the documentary evdience which helps explain its actions.

Background

Between the Balkan Wars and the Sarajevo crisis, Russo-German relations went from bad to worse. Russia reacted to a German move in 1913 to expand its army by embarking on a massive rearmament programme itself — one which would ensure Russia would never again be threatened by Germany.

This turning point in Russo-German relations led Kaiser William II to remark in February 1914:

(A) 'Russo-(German) relations are dead once and for all. We have become enemies.'

The German military shared similar fears. In May 1914 Moltke the German Chief of General Staff speaking to Foreign Secretary Jagow declared (in Jagow's words):

(B) 'The prospects for the future greatly depressed him. In two or three years, Russia will have completed her armaments programme. The military superiority of our foes will then be so great that he had no idea how we should overcome them. For the time being, we were still a match for them to some degree. In his opinion, the sole remaining option was to wage preventive war, to strike the enemy while we still had some chance of surviving the struggle.'

The Sarajevo Crisis

When the Sarajevo affair blew up, the German leadership felt they had to back Austria in its action against Serbia whatever the costs.

Bethmann-Hollwegg, the German Chancellor summed up Germany's position to his secretary on 6 July:

(C) 'The Entente knows that Germany is 'absolutely paralysed'. Austria is becoming ever weaker and less mobile. Russia's military strength is growing rapidly. The secret reports of Anglo-Russian naval discussions indicate the serious possibility of an English attempt to land forces in Pomerania in case of war. If Germany failed to provide support, then Austria-Hungary will approach the Western powers, whose arms are open, and we will lose our last military ally.'

The Plan

To cope with the Sarajevo affair, Bethmann-Hollwegg devised a plan. Germany would pledge its total support for Austria's plan to punish Serbia for the assassination. Moreover, Germany would urge Austria to make war on Serbia immediately.

If Austria crushed Serbia while the assassination was still on everyone's mind then Russia might not intervene. Then while the other entente powers were pondering what to do, Germany could sweet talk them around into accepting a peaceful settlement.

Indeed, if it all worked out as planned, Austria and Germany would be strengthened at the expense of Russia and Pan Slavism.

The Kaiser shared Bethmann-Hollwegg's views on how the Russians would react to an Austrian attack on Serbia. In early July the Kaiser explained to a member of his naval staff:

> (D) 'The intervention by Russia was unlikely because the Tsar will not lend his support to royal assassins and because Russia is, at the present moment, militarily and financially totally unprepared for war.'

On 18 July, Foreign Secretary Von Jagow outlined the goals of the German leadership to the German ambassador in London:

> (E) 'We must see to it that the conflict between Austria and Serbia is localised. Whether or not this succeeds depends first on Russia and second on the restraining influence of her Entente partners. The more determined Austria appears and the more energetically we support it, the more readily Russia will keep still. . . . France and England also do not want war now. According to all competent analyses, Russia will be ready for war in a few years. Then the number of its soldiers will crush us; then it will have completed construction of its Baltic fleet and strategic railways. In the meantime, our group will grow ever weaker. The Russians are well aware of this, and therefore desire nothing but peace and quiet for a few more years. . . . If the conflict cannot be localised, and Russia attacks Austria, then that is our *causus foederis*. At that point, we cannot abandon Austria. For we would then stand in an isolation that could hardly be called proud. I do not want a preventive war, but if war there will be, we cannot shirk it.'

The Plan Fails

The Austrians upset Bethmann-Hollwegg's plan by delaying their attack on Serbia. They sent their ultimatum to Serbia almost three weeks after the Germans had promised the Austrians their total support and four weeks after the assassinations at Sarajevo.

Once it became apparent the Bethmann-Hollwegg plan was going wrong and Russia was going to intervene, the military became more and more agitated. On 29 July Moltke wrote to Bethmann-Hollwegg:

(F) '(Russia) announces that she intends to mobilise when Austria advances into Serbia as she cannot permit the destruction of Serbia by Austria. . . . (Russia) has been getting herself so ready for war, that when she actually issues her mobilisation orders, she will be prepared to move her armies forward in a few days. . . .

'According to information at hand, France also appears to be taking measures preparatory to an eventual mobilisation. It is apparent that France and Russia are moving hand in hand as far as regards their preparations.

'Thus when the collision between Austria and Russia becomes inevitable. Germany will also mobilise, and will be prepared to take up the fight on two fronts.

' . . . it is of the greatest importance to ascertain as soon as possible whether Russia and France intend to let it come to a war with Germany. The further the preparations of our neighbours are carried, the quicker they will be able to complete their mobilisation. Thus the military situation is becoming from day to day more unfavourable to us, and can, if our prospective opponents prepare themselves further, lead to fateful consequences for us.'

On 30 July the Russians began to mobilise. On 1 August the Germans declared war on Russia and put the Schlieffen Plan into action. A European War was now inevitable.

Responsibility

Looking back in 1919, Jagow noted that he hoped to the very end:

(G) 'That a general war could be avoided. But I cannot deny that (when) this proved impossible, the memory of Moltke's remarks of late May 1914 that 'there was nothing left but to wage a preventive war while we could still withstand it to some degree' gave me a measure of confidence of a positive outcome.'

Bethmann-Hollwegg told a journalist in February 1915:

(H) 'When one discusses the responsibility for this war, we must honestly recognise that we too deserve our share of the blame.'

In 1917, in retirement, Bethmann-Hollwegg confessed to a Reichstag member:

(I) 'This war rages inside me. I continually ask myself if it could have been avoided, what I could have done. All nations bear responsibility for it; Germany too shares a great part of the blame. . . . In a certain sense it was a preventive war. But when war was hanging over us, when in two years it would have been even more dangerous and inescapable, and when the military says 'now, it is still possible without being defeated, but not in two years!'

ACTIVITIES

1. Why did Russo-German relations deteriorate so badly after the Balkan Wars? (A)

2. Why were the German military so concerned about Russia? (B)

3. Why did Bethmann-Hollwegg feel Germany had to support Austria in its dealings with Serbia following Sarajevo? (C)

4. How did the German leadership hope to turn the Sarajevo crisis to its advantage?

5. Why did the German leadership feel the Russian's were unlikely to intervene? (E) (D)

6. What did the success of the German plan depend upon? In your opinion was this a realistic expectation? (E)

7. What evidence is there that the Germans were prepared to risk a continental war should their attempts to localise the conflict in the Balkans fail? (E)

8. Why was Moltke so agitated by 29 July? (F)

9. What share of the responsibility were Jagow and Bethmann-Hollwegg prepared to accept? (G) (H)

10. *Talking point:* Historians who accept Germany's responsibility for the outbreak of war in 1914 have offered three basic explanations:

(i) Some, especially the German, Fritz Fischer claim that Germany deliberately provoked war with Russia, France and Britain in order to achieve world domination.

(ii) Others argue that Germany wanted war because she felt encircled and threatened by British naval power and by the Russian military expansion. The German generals decided that a 'preventive war' for survival, was necessary, and that it must take place before the end of 1914; after that Russia would be too strong.

(iii) Still others claim that Germany did not want a major war at all; the Kaiser and Chancellor Bethmann-Hollwegg believed a strong line in support of Austria would frighten the Russians into remaining neutral — a sad miscalculation if true.

Which of these explanations or combination of explanations seems to fit in with the evidence you have studied?

11. Write an essay of about 250-300 words on how far Germany was responsible for the outbreak of the First World War?

12 – Summing Up: What Caused the War and Who Was to Blame?

In this unit we will look at two different ways of looking at the causes of the First World War.

(A) *Here is a viewpoint which argues there were four basic or fundamental causes for the First World War.*

1. Nationalism

One of the forces making for trouble was extreme nationalism. This was a very powerful emotion. People who fell under its spell were willing to take any action to help their own nation, regardless of its effects on others. To promote their nation's interests, they were even ready to start wars.

Nationalism inspired Bismarck's war with France and the German seizure of Alsace-Lorraine. Relations between France and Germany suffered badly as a result. French nationalists could not rest as long as other Frenchmen were under the rule of the Germans. They preached a war of revenge to regain the 'lost provinces'.

Nationalism also led to rivalries in the Balkan Peninsula. Russia stirred up the Slavs in order to extend its influence there. It also supported the claims of the little kingdom of Serbia, which dreamed of uniting all the South Slavs under its rule. These actions aroused the leaders of Austria-Hungary. They realised that their country would fall apart if the millions of Slav subjects broke away.

Comment – Without doubt extreme nationalism was a potentially explosive force. It lay at the root of the quarrel between Austria and Serbia which finally exploded into war following Sarajevo. Nationalism however does not explain how a Balkan affair, escalated into a world war.

2. Colonial and Trade Rivalry

Imperialism (the building of overseas empires) also led to frequent quarrels among the powers. Disputes over colonies and commerce were a constant threat to peace during the late nineteenth and early twentieth centuries.

Comment – There is no denying colonial rivalry produced friction between the powers yet there is very little evidence to support the notion that colonial rivalry was a fundamental cause of the war. Britain's fiercest colonial rivals were France and Russia yet these three powers managed to settle their differences and fought on the same side during the war. Colonial rivalry may in fact have acted as a safety valve — diverting attention and energy away from European problems.

While Britain and Germany were trade rivals they were also very important customers for each others products. German manufacturers didn't need a war to achieve economic mastery. As one leading German industrialist remarked in 1913: 'Give us three or four more years of peace and Germany will be the unchallenged economic master of Europe'.

3. Militarism

Another threat to peace arose from the existence of large armies and navies. Leaders of the armed forces insisted that preparing for war was the only way to insure peace. As long as a nation was strong, they said, the nation would be able to defend itself successfully.

Nationalists, imperialists, and the makers of armaments supported these arguments. The result was an arms race. Each power kept building up its armed forces. Each was trying to have a bigger and deadlier war machine than its rivals.

Comment – Large armies and navies in themselves do not cause wars. They may in fact be deterrents. Naval rivalry between Britain and Germany however, was a major source of friction prior to the war.

Far more dangerous than armies and navies themselves were the mobilisation plans of the great powers. The German Schlieffen Plan in particular reduced the time available for negotiation in a crisis to virtually nil. Once actioned in August 1914, European war became inevitable.

4. The System of Alliances

Nations also sought to increase their strength by gaining allies. Europe was criss-crossed by rival systems of military alliances. These alliances were dangerous because they increased suspicion and fear. Moreover, they meant that a war between two nations was likely to involve many others.

Comment – The alliance system did not make European war inevitable. A number of previous crises had been solved without a major war.

The alliances were not as binding as is sometimes made out. France had not backed Russia over Bosnia in 1908. Austria did nothing to help Germany in its attempts to win Morocco from France. Despite being a member of the Triple Alliance, Italy remained neutral in 1914 and only went to war alongside the entente powers in 1915.

Another way of looking at the causes of the First World War is to focus on the question of national responsibility. In other words which country or countries were most responsible?

(B) *Below is an imaginary discussion between a group of historians. They are debating which power or powers was responsible for the outbreak of war.*

Speaker 1: Germany was responsible for starting World War I. It was Germany who seized Alsace and Lorraine in 1870. Germany started the naval race. German stupidity sparked off the First Moroccan crisis. This in turn led to the formation of the Triple Entente. While Germany did not start the Bosnian crisis in 1908, it did threaten Russia with war. Again in 1911 it was Germany who blundered by sending a gunboat to Agadir. In the July crisis of 1914 Austria would never have declared war on Serbia without German backing. Finally it was the German Schlieffen plan which pushed Europe into war.

Speaker 2: That's hardly fair. The war was sparked off by the assassination of Archduke Ferdinand. Serbia must take much of the blame for this. After all it was the Serbians who were stirring up trouble among the Southern Slavs.

Speaker 3: I agree. But Russia must share the blame with Serbia. Russia was also stirring up the Slavs, and Serbia would never have been as troublesome if she did not have Russian support. Furthermore, it was the Russian mobilisation in July 1914 which caused the Germans to mobilise and declare war.

Speaker 4: Yes, but Russia would never have mobilised if Austria had not declared war on Serbia. Remember, Austria was determined to crush Serbia once and for all. Therefore Austria must take the blame.

Speaker 5: What about France? During the July crisis France never ever bothered to try and stop the Russians from mobilising. And France's ambassador in Russia repeatedly urged the Russian's to take a strong stand against Austria and Germany.

Speaker 6: Britain also might have stopped the war. A strong warning to Germany in the early days of the July crisis, that England would fight alongside France and Russia in a war, might have made Germany see sense.

ACTIVITIES

1. Read through (A) carefully. Then rank the basic causes from 1-4 using Chart 1. 1 will indicate the most important cause, 4 will be the least important cause. In the reasons column explain why you ranked them in the order you chose.

2. Complete Chart 2 using (B) and your own knowledge. In the blame column use the key provided. In the ranking column number 1 will indicate the country most to blame, 6 will indicate the country least to blame. In the reasons column explain why you ranked them in the order you chose.

CHART 1 — THE BASIC CAUSES

Causes	Ranking	Reasons
Nationalism		
Colonial & Trade Rivalry		
Militarism		
Alliance System		

CHART 2 — WHOSE FAULT WAS THE WAR?

Countries	Blame (see key)	Ranking	Reasons
Germany			
Serbia			
Russia			
Austria			
France			
Britain			

KEY

S.B. — Solely to Blame
L.B. — Large Share of the Blame
S.S.B. — Small Share of the Blame
F.B. — Free from Blame

1871	January	German Empire proclaimed		February	HMS *Dreadnought* launched
1873	October	Three Emperors League between Germany, Austria-Hungary and Russia formed (dead by 1878)	1907	August	Anglo-Russian Entente completes Triple Entente
1879	October	Austro-German Dual Alliance	1908	September	Buchlau Conference
1881	June	Three Emperors League revived		October	Austria-Hungary annexes Bosnia-Herzegovinia
1882	May	Triple Alliance between Germany, Austria-Hungary and Italy	1909	March	German ultimatum to Russia ends Bosnian Crisis
1887	June	Three Emperors League lapses. Reinsurance Treaty between Germany and Russia	1911	1 July	Arrival of German gunboat *Panther* at Agadir provokes Second Moroccan Crisis
1888	June	Wilhelm II becomes Emperor of Germany		21 July	Lloyd George warns Germany in Mansion House speech
1890	March	Bismarck resigns as Chancellor of Germany	1912	October	First Balkan War begins
1894	January	Franco-Russian Entente	1913	May	Treaty of London ends First Balkan War
1898	March	Reichstag approves Tirpitz's First Navy Act		June	Second Balkan War begins
1899	October	Outbreak of Boer War		August	Treaty of Bucharest ends Second Balkan War
1900	June	Reichstag approves Second Navy Act	1914	28 June	Sarajevo assassinations
1902	May	Anglo-Japanese Alliance		23 July	Austria-Hungary ultimatum to Serbia
	June	Treaty of Vereeniging ends Boer War		28 July	Austria-Hungary declares war on Serbia
1904	February	Russo-Japanese War begins		30 July	Russia mobilises
	April	Entente Cordiale between Britain and France		1 August	Germany declares war on Russia and mobilises
1905	March	Kaiser's visit to Tangiers sparks off First Moroccan Crisis		3 August	Germany declares war on France
1906	January	Algeciras Conference following Moroccan Crisis		4 August	Great Britain declares war on Germany

SOME PROMINENT PERSONALITIES

This list is designed to help you identify personalities you may come across in your further reading. As such it includes personalities not mentioned in this book.

Aehrenthal, Count Lexa von — Austro-Hungarian Minister for Foreign Affairs, 1906-1912

Alexander II — Emperor of Russia, 1855-81

Alexander III — Emperor of Russia, 1881-94

Asquith, Herbert — British Prime Minister, 1905-15

Berchtold, Count Leopold von — Austro-Hungarian Minister for Foreign Affairs, 1912-15

Bethmann-Hollwegg, Theobald von — German Chancellor, 1909-17

Bismarck, Otto von — German Chancellor, 1871-90

Bülow, Prince Bernhard von — German Chancellor, 1900-09

Caprivi, Count Georg Leo — German Chancellor, 1890-1904

Conrad, Franz, Count von Hotzendorf — Chief of the Austrian General Staff, 1912-17

Churchill, Winston — First Lord of the (British) Admiralty, 1911-15

Delcassé, Theophile — French Minister for Foreign Affairs, 1898-1905

Edward VII — King of Great Britain and Ireland, 1901-1910

Fisher, Sir John — First Sea Lord, 1903-09

Franz, Ferdinand, Archduke — Heir to the throne of Austria-Hungary

Franz, Joseph I — Emperor of Austria and Hungary, 1848-1916

George V — King of Great Britain and Ireland, 1910-36

Goschen, Sir Edward — British Ambassador in Germany

Grey, Sir Edward — British Foreign Secretary, 1905-16

Hohenlohe-Schillingsfürst, Prince Chlodwig zu — German Chancellor, 1894-1900

Izvolsky, Alexander Petrovich — Russian Minister for Foreign Affairs, 1906-10

Jagow, Goltlieb von — German Secretary of State for Foreign Affairs, 1913-16

Kiderlen-Waechter, Alfred von — German Minister of Foreign Affairs, 1910-12

Lichnowsky, Prince Karl Max — German Ambassador in Britain, 1912-14

Lloyd George, David — British Chancellor of the Exchequer, 1908-13

Moltke, Helmuth J.L. von — Chief of the German General Staff, 1906-14

Nicholas II — Emperor of Russia, 1894-1917

Pasić, Nokola — Serbian Prime Minister, 1910-18

Poincaré, Raymond — French Prime Minister, 1911-13; President, 1913-20

Princip, Gavrilo — Serbian conspirator who assassinated Archduke Ferdinand and his wife

Sazonov, Sergei Dimitrievich — Russian Minister for Foreign Affairs, 1910-16

Schlieffen, Alfred — German Chief of the General Staff, 1891-1905. Author of Schlieffen plan

Tirpitz, Alfred von — German Admiral and Navy Minister, 1898-1916

Viviani, René — French Prime Minister and Minister for Foreign Affairs, 1914-15

Wilhelm II — German Kaiser, 1888-1918

FURTHER READING

The following are recommended because they are sound, clear and concise.

Duncan MacIntyre, *The Great War, Causes and Consequences* (Blackie, 1979)

Joachim Remak, *The Origins of World War I, 1871-1914* (Holt Rinehart and Winston 1967)

Bernadotte E. Schmitt, *The Origins of the First World War* (Historical Association Pamphlet G39, 1958)

L.C.F. Turner, *Origins of the First World War* (Arnold, 1970)

L.C.F. Turner, *The Coming of the First World War* (Warne, 1969)

General Texts

There are many good general texts with relevant chapters. Two of the best are:

James Joll, *Europe Since 1870* (Penguin, 1976)

J.M. Roberts, *Europe 1880-1945* (Longman, 1965)

Sketch Maps

Martin Gilbert, *First World War Atlas* (Weidenfeld & Nicolson, 1970)

Some Interesting Books to Read

A.J.P. Taylor, *How Wars Begin* (Hamish Hamilton, 1979)

G.M. Thomson, *The Twelve Days 24 July to 4 August 1914* (Hutchinson, 1964)

Barbara Tuchman, *August 1914* (Papermac, 1980)

Teacher Reference

The above books should be supplemented by:

H.W. Koch, ed., *The Origins of the First World War* (Macmillan, 1972)

V.R. Berghahn, *Germany and the Approach of War* (Macmillan, 1973)

Richard Bosworth, *Italy and the Approach of the First World War* (Macmillan, 1983)

John F.V. Keiger, *France and the Origins of the First World War* (Macmillan, 1983)

D.C.B. Lieven, *Russia and the Origins of the First World War* (Macmillian, 1983)

SOURCES

1 – The Roots Of Strife
(A) *Punch,* 27 September 1873.
(B) Mary Evans Picture Library.
(C) Adapted by author from 1981 University Entrance History paper.
(D) B. Tuchman, *August 1914,* Macmillan Papermac, p.40.
(E) Purnells *History of the Twentieth Century.*

2 – Germany's Quest For World Power
(A) *Table 1.* U.S.A. *Historical Statistics of the U.S.A.* Bureau of the Census, 1961.
Other countries, B.R. Mitchell, *European Historical Statistics 1750-1970,* Macmillan Press, 1975.
Table 2. W.W. Rostow, *The World Economy: History and Prospect,* University of Texas Press, 1978, Table 11-2, pp.52-53.
Table 3. Ibid, Table 11-8, pp.70-4.
(B) Cited in H.W. Koch ed., *The Origins of the First World War,* Macmillan, p.80 and p.43.
(C) John Hamer, *The Twentieth Century,* Macmillan Education, 1980, p.14.
(D) D. MacIntyre, *The Great War,* Blackie, 1919, p.35.
(E) Cited, F. Fischer, *War of Illusions,* Chatto and Windus, 1975.

3 – The End of British Isolation
(A) Punch, 12 April 1905.
(B) Punch, 11 October 1905.
(C) Punch, 1901.
(D) (i) cited, Michael Balfour, *The Kaiser and His Times,* Cresset, 1964.
(ii) cited, F. Fischer, *Ibid.*
(iii) cited, F. Fischer, *Ibid.*
(iv) cited, F. Fischer, *Ibid.*
(E) Compiled by author.

4 – The Balkan Powderkeg
(A) L'Assiette an Beurre.
(B) Compiled by author.
(C) Harry Mills, *Twentieth Century History in Focus,* Macmillan Education, 1983.
(D) Cited, Purnells *History of the 20th Century, 20th Century Scrapbook,* 1906-1908, p.72.

5 – The Arms Race
(A) Figures from J.I. McManus, *Federation and the Modern World,* John Wiley & Sons, Sydney, 1975, p.39.
(B) M. Balfour, *The Kaiser and His Times,* Cresset Press, 1964.
(C) Imperial War Museum.
(D) Imperial War Museum.
(E) Compiled by author.
(F) Compiled by author.
(G) Purnells *History of The 20th Century,* BPC Publishing, 1968, p.185.
(H) Radio Times Hulton Picture Library.

6 – The Will To Make War
(A) Cited, Purnells *History of The Twentieth Century,* B.P.C. Publishing 1968, No. 7, Scrapbook Section.
(B) Cited, J. Remak, *The Origins of World War I,* Holt Rhinehart and Winston, 1967, p.84.
(C) Copied from D. McIntyre, *The Great War,* Blackie, 1979.
(D) Mansell Collection.

7 – The Agadir Incident 1911
(A) Central Bibliothek, Zurich.
(B) *Punch,* 2 August 1911.
(C) (i) Cited, F. Fischer, *War of Illusions,* Chatto and Windus, 1975.
(ii) Cited J. Terraine, *Impacts of War,* pp.31-32.

8 – War Clouds Over The Balkans
(A) Harry Mills, *Twentieth Century World History in Focus,* Macmillan Education, 1979.
(B) *Ibid.*
(C) Mansell Collection.
(D) Mansell Collection.

9 – Planning For Victory
(A) Harry Mills, *Twentieth Century World History in Focus,* Macmillan Education, 1979.
(B) Imperial War Museum.
(C) A.J.P. Taylor, *How Wars Begin,* Hamish Hamilton, 1979, p.117.
(D) B. Tuchman, *August 1914,* Constable London, 1962, pp.86-81.
(E) Compiled by author.

10 – The Final Crisis
(A) Radio Times Hulton Picture Library.
(B) *Punch,* 1914.
(C) British post card of 1914, copied from Parnells *History of The 20th Century,* B.P.C. Publishing, 1968, No. 16, Scrapbook Section.
(D) Kladderadatsch.
(E) A.J.P. Taylor, *How Wars Begin,* Hamish Hamilton, 1979, p.117.
(F) G.M. Thomson, *The Twelve Days,* Hutchinson, 1964, pp.151, 152, 161.

11 – German Leadership and the July Crisis
(A) Cited in W. Carr, *A History of Germany 1815-1945,* Edward Arnold, 1979, p.218.
(B) Cited in Andreas Hillgruber, *Germany and the Two World Wars,* Harvard University Press, Cambridge, Massachusetts, 1981, p.29.
(C) *Ibid,* p.32.
(D) Cited, V.R. Berghahn, *Germany and the Approach of War in 1914,* Macmillan, 1973, p.189.
(E) Hillgruber, *Ibid,* p.33.
(F) Imanuel Geiss, German Foreign Policy, 1871-1914, Routledge Kegan Paul, 1976, pp.214-215.
(G) Hillgruber, *Ibid,* p.34.
(H) *Ibid,* pp.39-40.
(I) *Ibid.*

12 – Summing Up
(A) Main text adapted from Sydney H. Zbel, and Sydney Schwartz, *Past to Present: A World History,* The Macmillan Company, 1960, New York, pp.541-542.
(B) Compiled by author.